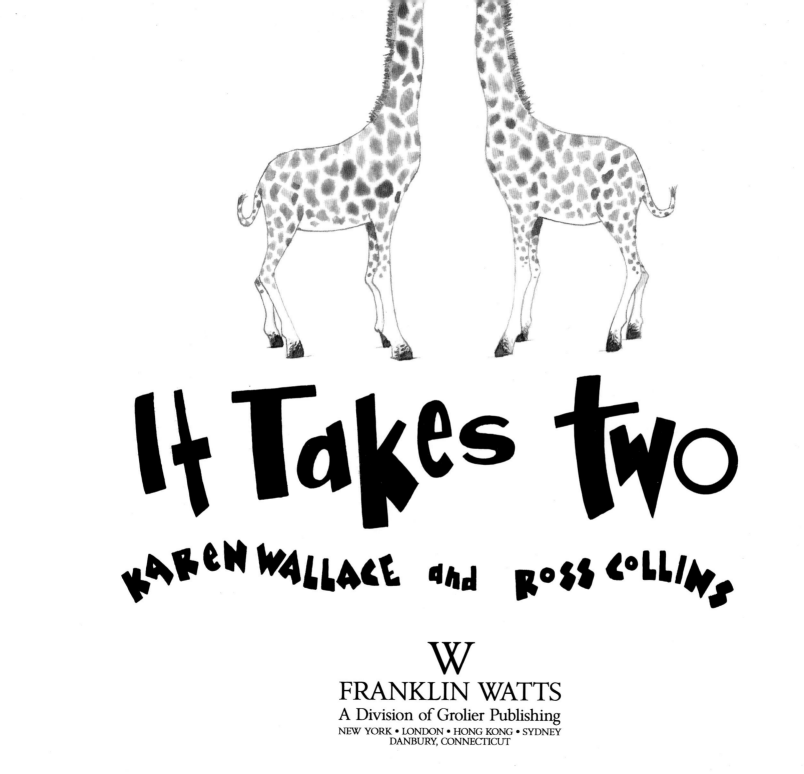

It Takes Two

KAREN WALLACE and ROSS COLLINS

W
FRANKLIN WATTS
A Division of Grolier Publishing
NEW YORK • LONDON • HONG KONG • SYDNEY
DANBURY, CONNECTICUT

This is a book about twos. It's about hes and shes.

2

Because that's how life begins. It Takes Two!

Sometimes he is much bigger than she is.

A bull elephant seal is as long as
a big car and weighs more than
a small tractor.
He's famous for his bad temper.

A cow elephant seal is smaller
and much gentler, too!

Sometimes **she** is much bigger than **he** is.

An angler fish lives deep down in the sea. Her mate is only a bit bigger than a tadpole.

6

A pink crab spider hardly notices
her tiny partner. Would you
if you were her?

A queen termite lays 30,000 eggs a day.
She is as long as your hand
and so **FAT** she cannot move.

A king termite is as tiny as a wasp.

Some animal pairs
look completely different
which is how **she** notices
him in the first place.

How could she ignore him? This mandrill's face almost glows in the dark!

Sometimes **he** makes sounds to send messages to her. **He** hopes that **she** is listening.

A howler monkey

HOWLS

Phoo

A kakapo stands in the middle of the forest and makes a sound like blowing over the top of an empty bottle.

zzz z zz z z z zzz zz z z z zz zz z zz z z zz z z z z

A grasshopper rubs his legs together.

Sometimes he leaves smells to send messages and mark his territory. He hopes that she will notice.

A skunk's scent is soooooo smelly he uses it to send messages and also to protect himself from danger.

A ring-tailed lemur does a handstand and sprays a tree with his scent.

DOGS OFTEN CHOOSE LAMP POSTS TO LEAVE THEIR MESSAGE.

He and she fireflies send their messages at night.

They
FLASH
to find
a mate.

15

Sometimes **he** makes the nest. When it's ready **she** lays her eggs and looks after them.

A weaverbird is an amazing nest builder. He knots pieces of grass and weaves them into different shapes. Some nests are round with a hole on one side. Some nests even have tunnels.

A wren builds several nests.
He picks the strangest places.
She chooses her favorite
and pads it
with feathers.

A little ringed plover
scrapes a hollow in
bare ground.
She then lines it
with pebbles
and stalks.

17

Sometimes when **she** lays the eggs, **he** keeps them in a special place and looks after them.

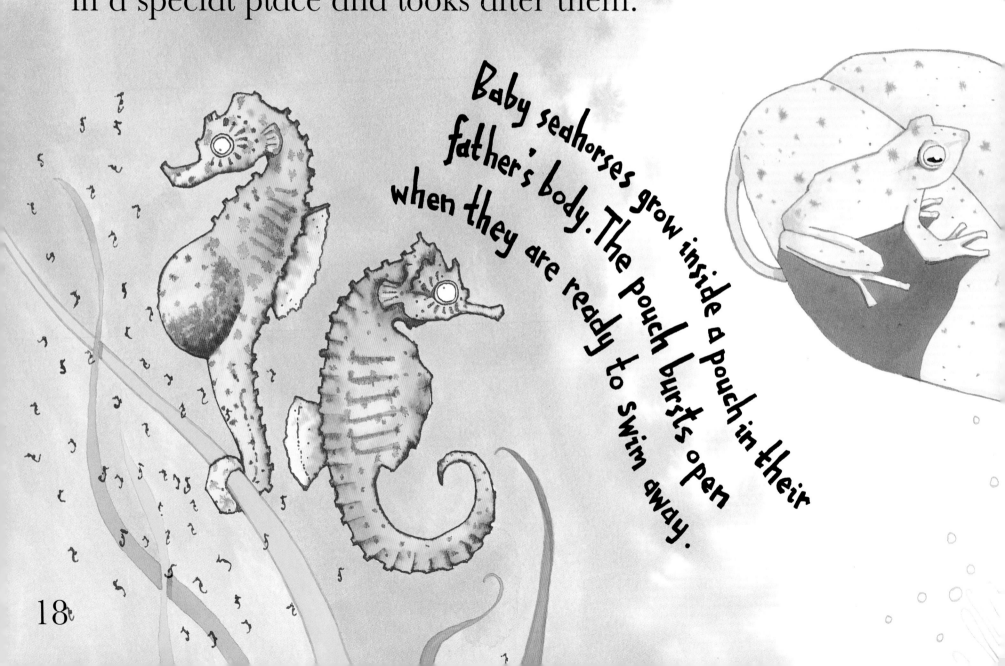

Baby seahorses grow inside a pouch in their father's body. The pouch bursts open when they are ready to swim away.

A glass frog
hides with
his eggs in
the leaves above
jungle streams.
When the eggs
hatch, the
tadpoles
drop
into
the
water
SPloosh.

An emperor penguin
holds the egg
on his
feet
and keeps
it warm against
his body.
For two months
he stands
in the
FReeZiNg cold.

19

Sometimes he builds the nest and he looks after the eggs. She only lays them!

A Japanese fighting fish builds a nest of bubbles. He carries each egg up to the nest before she has a chance to eat them!

A lily-trotter bird makes a floating nest on a swamp. He hatches the eggs and looks after the chicks.

An Australian brush turkey buries the eggs in a nest that looks like a compost heap. If they get too hot, he uncovers them. If they get too cold, he covers them up.

21

Many birds share the work and stay together for life.
He and **she** even look the same!

Albatrosses take turns to fly thousands of miles to find food for their chick.

Blue-footed boobies share the job of keeping their egg warm.

A father hornbill seals his mate into a hollow tree with mud while she sits on the eggs.

He brings her food and pushes it through a tiny hole.

23

Mammal babies suck their mothers' milk, so it is not surprising that **she** does most of the work as they grow.

A mother raccoon teaches her babies to wash the river clams they like to eat.

A mother chimpanzee picks fleas from her daughter's fur to keep her healthy.

Cheetah kittens are born blind and helpless. Their mother feeds them and later teaches them to hunt for themselves.

25

Not all mammals leave the job of looking after the young to the mother. Sometimes he helps out a little.

A father fox brings food to the cubs when they are too young to catch it themselves.

Marmosets and tamarinds almost always have twins so the father helps carry the babies.

A father hyena looks after his young when their mother is hunting.

27

If you think this book is just about animals, YOU ARE WRONG!

IT TAKES TWO!

Helpful information

Angler fish (page 6) the tiny male is like a worm. When he finds his mate, he attaches himself and stays there.

Cheetah (page 25) a mother cheetah must protect her cubs from male cheetahs.

Chimpanzee (page 24) a mother also grooms her daughter to help form a special friendship between them.

Emperor penguin (page 19) while the male keeps the egg warm, the baby is growing inside.

Fireflies (pages 14-15) can flash because of a glowing chemical in their bodies.

Hatching (pages 18-19, 21, 22-23) a bird sits on its eggs to keep them warm, so the babies inside can grow and hatch from their shells.

Howler monkey (page 10) a howler monkey also howls to warn others of danger.

Kakapo (page 11) this rare New Zealand parrot is awake only at night.

Pink spider crab (page 7) the tiny male crab has to be very careful because his mate would eat him if she gets the chance.

Sea Horse (page 18) the female gives all her eggs to the male who keeps them inside his body until they are ready to be born.

To Willy Bullough with thanks — KW

For Charlie — RC

© 1997 Franklin Watts
First American Edition 1997 by
Franklin Watts, A division of Grolier Publishing
90 Sherman Turnpike, Danbury, CT 06816
Text © 1997 Karen Wallace
Illustrations © Ross Collins
Series editor: Paula Borton
Art director: Robert Walster
Consultant: Dr Jim Flegg
Printed in Singapore

Library of Congress Cataloging-in-Publication Data
Wallace, Karen.
        It takes two / Karen Wallace and Ross Collins. --
        1st American ed.
        p. cm. -- (Wonderwise)
    Summary : Examines courtship, mating, nesting, and caring for babies
        by various members of the animal kingdom.
        ISBN 0-531-14487-9 (hc). -- ISBN 0-531-15325-8 (pbk.)
        1. Courtship of animals -- Juvenile literature. 2. Sexual behavior in animals --
    Juvenile literature. 3. Parental behavior in animals -- Juvenile literature.
        [1.Animals--Courtship. 2. Sexual behavior in animals.
        3. Parental behavior in animals. 4. Animals--Habits and behavior.]--
        I. Collins, Ross II. Title. III. Series.
        QL761. W26   1997
        591- 56'2--dc21   97-13561
                                                                              CIP
                                                                               AC